A PICTURE TOUR OF

THE NATIONAL MUSEUM OF NATURAL HISTORY

Text by Robert D. Sullivan and Sue Voss
Special photography by Chip Clark

SMITHSONIAN INSTITUTION PRESS, WASHINGTON, D.C.

EXPLORE THE WORLD WITH US

The National Museum of Natural History displays the treasures of nature—nature that includes us as part of its wonderful living web. More than a century of careful collecting and research by scientists and scholars has resulted in an unsurpassed world collection. There are now over 100 million natural and cultural objects for your enjoyment and discovery in this museum, one of the fourteen museums in the great Smithsonian Institution complex.

You will find meteorites from outer space that help us understand the origins of our blue planet; sparkling crystals formed deep in the earth over millions of years; fossils that tell us of a different, earlier world when strange creatures swam, crawled, walked, and flew among plants and landscapes that stretch our imagination; and the material evidence of the emergence of our own species, the tool-making one, which steadily colonizes the earth and develops rich cultures and complex customs and beliefs.

The story told in the museum is about change. Ours is a changing earth, which spun out of a star out of a galaxy, and which cooled until today we ride a restless moving crust of continents and seas on an earth with a molten core. Early in this planet's life came a life force that evolved and diversified over 3.5 billion years, sometimes suffering huge destruction and then recovering, and today providing a rich pattern of species—from the delicacy of a tropical forest butterfly or the power of the blue whale, to the art and industry of humankind.

I hope you enjoy this souvenir of the National Museum of Natural History. As you wonder at its riches, remember that some of them are now disappearing through man-made changes, and wise stewardship is needed to pass them on to the children who are our successors.

Frank H. Talbot
Director

Opposite: A landmark in the Smithsonian Institution, the African elephant welcomes visitors at the museum's Mall entrance.
Preceding pages: Page 1. Master of deception, a South American emerald moth bears a striking resemblance to its lichen-covered background. *Pages 2-3.* Color shifts in this natural candelabra of elbaite, a variety of tourmaline, were caused by chemical changes in the solutions from which the crystals grew.
Pages 4-5. Sharks prowl in what might appear to be a modern snapshot, but this mural by artist Ely Kish flashes back to the Mesozoic Era, 230 to 65 million years ago, in the exhibit *Life in the Ancient Seas.*

THE LIVING WORLD

❧

FROM SO SIMPLE A BEGINNING ENDLESS FORMS MOST BEAUTIFUL AND MOST WONDERFUL HAVE BEEN, AND ARE BEING, EVOLVED.

❧

CHARLES DARWIN

DON'T BE SURPRISED IF EACH TIME YOU VISIT THE NATIONAL MUSEUM OF NATURAL HISTORY YOU DISCOVER SOMETHING NEW— SOMETHING YOU HADN'T KNOWN OR NOTICED BEFORE. THE MUSEUM MIMICS THE DIVERSITY OF THE NATURAL WORLD IT STUDIES: THERE IS ALWAYS SOMETHING NEW TO NOTICE OR KNOW.

DID YOU KNOW, FOR INSTANCE, THAT THERE ARE OVER 20,000 SPECIES OF BEES, OR THAT ORCHID POLLINATORS SHIMMER WITH THE SAME IRIDESCENT COLORS OF THE FLOWERS THEMSELVES? OR THAT BLUE WHALES STILL HAVE INTERNAL REMNANTS OF LEGS AND FEET IN THEIR TAILS, EVOLUTIONARY LEFTOVERS FROM DISTANT ANCESTORS THAT LIVED ON LAND? DON'T BE SURPRISED IF, BEYOND THE FACTS, RESEARCH, AND INTERPRETATION YOU DISCOVER HERE, YOUR MOST ENDURING MEMORY OF YOUR VISIT IS A SENSE OF WONDER AND AWE AT THE COMPLEXITY, ORDER, BEAUTY, AND EVEN MYSTERY, OF THE NATURAL WORLD. ✺

1

2

PRECEDING PAGES: White-tailed deer pause while browsing in a cypress swamp, in a North American Mammals hall diorama. 🦌

1. An adult walrus may reach 12 feet in length and weigh as much as 3000 pounds; arctic colonies may number 200 individuals.

2. In herds of African hartebeests, one or more individuals will stand sentry duty on the plains.

3. African buffalo graze on sub-Saharan open plains in this Mammals hall diorama.

4. The Russell's viper of Asia folds its fearsome fangs back except when striking.

3

4

5. Grizzly bears were once widespread in the West but today survive only in remote areas. **6.** Cougars are shown in Yellowstone Canyon in this diorama in the North American Mammals hall. **7.** An Indian tiger lunges as if to capture a deer. **8.** A life-size fiberglass model of a blue whale, the largest mammal and largest creature of any kind that has ever lived, dominates the Sea Life hall.

9. Bighorn sheep graze on grassy slopes in the Canadian Rockies and move onto rocky ledges to escape danger.

5

6

7

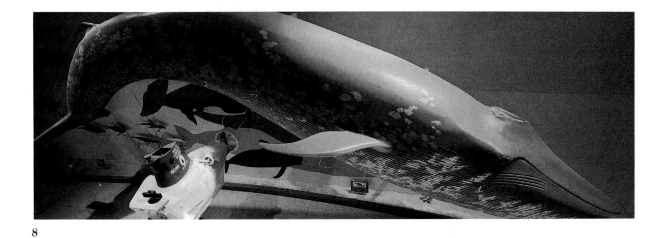

8

9

10. High in the Canadian Rockies, mountain goats forage on sparse timberline vegetation. **11.** Birds of the Antarctic include Emperor and Adelie penguins. **12.** Galapagos marine iguanas are the only living marine lizards. **13.** The vampire bat earns its common name by feeding on warm-blooded animals, sometimes including humans. **14.** The armadillo rolls up into a ball when threatened, protected by its hard bony plates.

15. An alligator patrols this diorama of the Florida Everglades, in the Reptiles and Amphibians hall.

10

11

12

13

14

15

16. A close-up reveals the structure of a peacock feather. **17.** The brilliant male scarlet tanager is one of many specimens in *Birds of the District of Columbia Region*, an exhibit that has helped generations of visitors identify local species. **18.** Accurate illustration has always been an essential part of research. This example from 1874 appeared in *A History of North American Birds* by Spencer Baird (the Smithsonian's second Secretary), Thomas Brewer, and Robert Ridgway.

19. Once America's most abundant bird, passenger pigeons were extinct in the wild by 1900. "Martha," the last survivor, died in captivity in 1914. **20.** Walled into her nest by mud for protection, a female rhinoceros hornbill receives food from her mate, in a diorama of a Borneo tropical forest. **21.** Ostrich chicks can keep up with their flightless, running parents within a month after hatching.

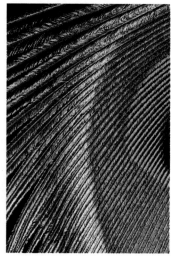

16

17

18

22. The museum's vast collection of eggs, stored behind the scenes, played a key role in research showing how DDT in the food chain caused some birds of prey to lay thin-shelled eggs.

19

20

21

22

23. The extinct shark behind these jaws was 40 feet long. Even the biggest of its living relatives, the great white shark, is only half this size.

24. Technicians monitor tanks and support equipment for the living Coral Reef, the first museum exhibit of its kind.   **25.** A Christmas tree worm lives in a tube on hard coral.
26. The clownfish usually lives symbiotically with a sea anemone, but in this aquarium has chosen a Pacific mushroom coral for its home.
27. A gray angelfish swims among hard coral and tubular sponges on a Caribbean reef.

23

24

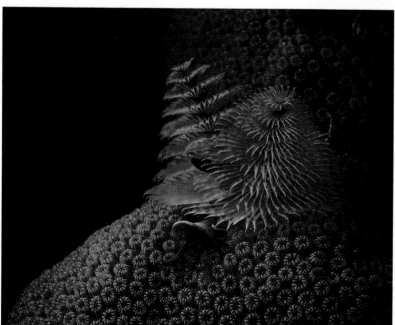

25

28. Because fishes lose color rapidly after death, an illustration often offers the best reference for study. This is an anemonefish. **29.** Some of the museum's most important fish illustrations were done as early as 1838; this stonefish was painted early this century.

26

28

29

27

30. Merging models, murals, and artifacts, the South America hall re-creates environments of the continent's native cultures, here an Amazonian rain forest. **31.** A crowned woodnymph hummingbird sips nectar and simultaneously pollinates Costa Rican heliconia flowers. In field research, museum zoologists, entomologists, and botanists jointly investigate plant-animal interactions. **32.** This Brazilian bamboo is only one of more than 4 million dried, pressed plant specimens maintained here in the National Herbarium. **33.** Museum botanists grow orchids and other plants from around the world in this greenhouse, for research on ecology and plant relationships and classification. **34.** This watercolor of American and kousa dogwoods accompanied a museum botanist's scientific publication; skillful illustration is important for describing and comparing species. **35.** Orchids from the Smithsonian's large greenhouse collection are often shown in the

30

31

32

lobby of the museum's Constitution Avenue entrance. **36.** Preserved plants or meticulous replicas are a key element in re-creating natural dioramas: here spruces, aspens, willows, and low heathers set a fall scene for a gathering of moose.

33

34

35

36

THE LIVING MEMORY

❧

THE MYRIAD PAST, IT ENTERS US AND DISAPPEARS.
EXCEPT THAT WITHIN IT SOMEWHERE, LIKE DIAMONDS,
EXIST THE FRAGMENTS THAT REFUSE TO BE CONSUMED.

❧

DENISE LEVERTOV

WHEN DID LIFE BEGIN? HOW DID LIVING SPECIES ORIGINATE AND WHY HAVE SOME DISAPPEARED? HOW CAN THE EARTH'S PAST HELP US PREDICT ITS FUTURE?

THE ANSWERS LIE IN FOSSILS. MUSEUM FIELD EXPEDITIONS HAVE SCRAPED, CHISELED, AND BRUSHED AWAY THE MANTLE OF TIME TO REVEAL DELICATE IMPRESSIONS AND MONUMENTAL MEMORIES OF LIFE'S PAST. WHETHER AWESOME DINOSAUR BONES OR A FLOWER'S FRAGILE TRACERY, EACH FOSSIL IS AN ORGANIC MOMENT CAPTURED IN STONE. FOSSIL MICROBES, OVER 800 MILLION YEARS OLD, ARE HERE IN *THE EARLIEST TRACES OF LIFE*; AND A 70-MILLION-YEAR-OLD MOSASAUR'S BITE IS FOREVER RECORDED IN AN AMMONITE'S SHELL IN *LIFE IN THE ANCIENT SEAS*.

FROM FOSSILS AS SMALL AS A POLLEN GRAIN OR AS LARGE AS A PETRIFIED TREE, YOU CAN UNRAVEL THE EARTH'S SHIFTING ECOLOGICAL HISTORY AND DISCOVER DYNAMIC PATTERNS OF CHANGE THAT STILL PROPEL US TOWARDS OUR FUTURE. 🍃

1

2

3

PRECEDING PAGES: This 50-million-year-old fossil flower from the shales of Colorado's Green River formation looks as if it might have been pressed yesterday. ❧

1. These creatures are modeled after fossils of 570-million-year-old soft-bodied organisms, some unlike any known plants or animals, found in Australia's Ediacara Hills. 2. A monument to an unknown animal that left tracks on a sandy sea floor half a billion years ago stands at the entrance to the fossil exhibits. 3. Even the fine bristles on which an ancient polychaete worm moved are exquisitely preserved in this Burgess Shale fossil. 4. In this imaginative scene from the "Tower of Time," a giant, clawed eurypterid menaces other invertebrates from ancient seas, 500 to 400 million years ago. 5. This scene is based on fossils from the remarkable 520-million-year-old Burgess Shale of British Columbia. 6. A 3.5-billion-year-old stromatolite made by blue-green algae or bacteria provides the oldest evidence of life.

4

5

6

7. *Dimetrodon*, which lived somewhere between 280 and 250 million years ago, was not a dinosaur, but a "mammal-like" reptile.
8. A mural in the Fossil Mammals hall crowds many grazers and predators into an idealized scene of Miocene grasslands. **9.** Dinosaur *Albertosaurus* confronts *Tyrannosaurus*; which will eat *Edmontosaurus*?

7

9

10. Almost as ferocious-looking as *Tyrannosaurus*, *Antrodemus* was an active hunter and could attack other dinosaurs as large as *Stegosaurus*. **11.** *Tyrannosaurus* terrorizes a smaller dinosaur, while an early mammal lurks in the foreground in this "Tower of Time" scene.

10

11

12. Deceptively flowerlike, these crinoids were actually animals. **13.** Chemical changes after burial produced this pearly fossil of an ammonite, an extinct relative of the nautilus.

14. A mosasaur nabs an ammonite; like the dinosaurs, mosasaurs and other giant marine reptiles died out 65 million years ago. **15.** A long-lost relative of insects and other arthropods, this trilobite lived in ancient seas 395 to 345 million years ago.

12

13

14

16. Scenes from seas past come to life in this life-size diorama of a 250-million-year-old reef.
17. Bony fishes and coiled ammonites swam Mesozoic seas, 230 to 65 million years ago.

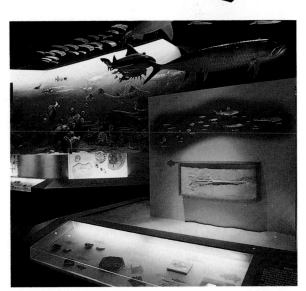

15

16

17

18. The skeleton of *Diplodocus* looms over the Dinosaur hall, while *Quetzalcoatlus northropi* soars in the background. 19. These *Plateosaurus* dinosaurs still shared the land mostly with other non-dinosaur reptiles 220 million years ago. 20. This huge placoderm fish prowled the sea floor about 350 million years ago. 21. The largest of the horned dinosaurs, *Triceratops* was also one of the last to become extinct.

22. This papier-mache *Stegosaurus*, constructed in 1904, is accurate in all but one detail: we now know that its largest pair of plates should be behind the hip joint, not in front.

18

19

20

21

22

23

23. In forests that grew after the last ice age, the Irish elk's enormous antlers were a hindrance—this elk became extinct about 11,000 years ago. **24.** Beneath the giant ground sloth's forelimbs, a glyptodont displays its fortresslike armor. This harmless vegetarian became extinct about 23,000 years ago. **25.** Only 14,000 years ago, this sabertoothed cat became mired in the tarpits of Rancho La Brea, California.

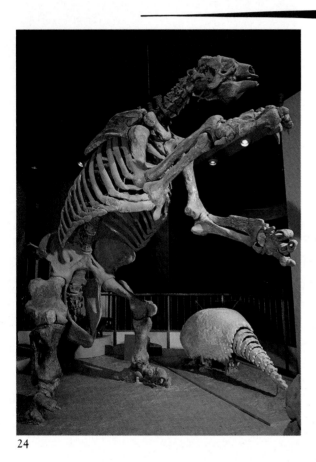

24

25

26

26. The most common animal found in California's Rancho La Brea tarpits, the dire wolf was larger than modern wolves but slower and less intelligent.   **27.** Now extinct, the 20-foot-tall South American giant ground sloth spread into North America about 4 to 3 million years ago.   **28.** An extinct elephant, the woolly mammoth once abounded in the glacial conditions of North America and northern Eurasia.

27

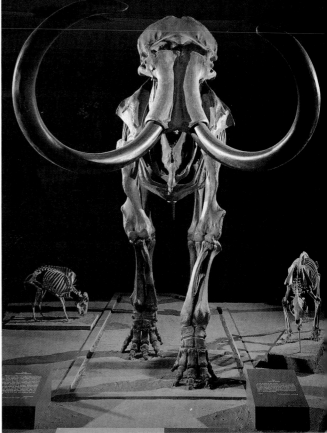

28

THE EMERGING EARTH

❧

THIS GRAND SHOW IS ETERNAL.
IT IS ALWAYS SUNRISE SOMEWHERE: THE DEW IS NEVER
ALL DRIED AT ONCE.

❧

JOHN MUIR

IT MAY BE HARD TO IMAGINE THAT SOMETHING AS PERMANENT AS A MOUNTAIN CHANGES CONTINUALLY, THAT SOMETHING AS PONDEROUS AS A CONTINENT FLOATS ACROSS THE OCEAN FLOOR. ON THE EARTH'S SCALE, ALL FORM IS BUT A MOMENT'S HESITATION ABOUT TO BECOME SOMETHING ELSE.

MUSEUM GEOLOGISTS ANALYZE THE EMERGING EARTH, SEEKING PATTERNS, DIRECTIONS. WHERE MIGHT THE NEXT EARTHQUAKE OCCUR? HOW MIGHT VOLCANIC ACTIVITY AFFECT HAWAII? HOW WOULD RISING SEA LEVELS AFFECT COASTAL COMMUNITIES?

AS YOU EXPLORE THE MUSEUM, YOU'LL DISCOVER EVIDENCE OF THE FIRST LIFE, TOUCH A METEORITE THAT HOLDS CLUES TO THE ORIGINS OF THE UNIVERSE ITSELF, MARVEL AT MINERALS NATURALLY REFINED FROM ROCK TO BECOME CRYSTALS AS BEAUTIFUL AS ANY CUT GEMS. EXPERIENCING EVIDENCE OF THE EARTH'S CONSTANT CHANGE CAN LEAD TO UNDERSTANDING AND CARING ABOUT THIS PLANET'S UNCERTAIN FUTURE. ❧

1

2

3

PRECEDING PAGES: Volcanoes dot the landscape 3.5 billion years ago. Geologic forces still at work today were shaping the earth, as very early forms of life were emerging. 🐌

1. Lava from Mauna Ulu, the cone in the distance, cascades into the crater Alo'i on Hawaii in 1969. **2.** Seismograph measurements in the Geology hall monitor one part of the changing earth. **3.** This unique ring-shaped iron meteorite was used by the Spanish in Tucson as an anvil.

4. In polarized light, a thin section of a basaltic moon rock reveals colorful pyroxene crystals in darker glass matrix. **5.** An aggregate of pre-planetary dust, the 4.5-billion-year-old Murchison meteorite fell in Australia in 1969. **6.** This lunar basaltic volcanic specimen was collected from the Taurus-Littrow valley by the Apollo 17 crew.

4

5

6

7. This sample of fluorite is from the Elmwood mine, Smith County, Tennessee.   **8.** Spiky millerite crystals were deposited on hematite lining a cavity in the host rock.   **9.** In this polished slice from a phosphate nodule, the blue-green mineral is variscite.   **10.** Both of these minerals, microcline (or amazonite) and smoky quartz, probably grew simultaneously.
11. Malachite formed on azurite in this specimen from the famous Copper Queen mine in Bisbee, Arizona.

7

8

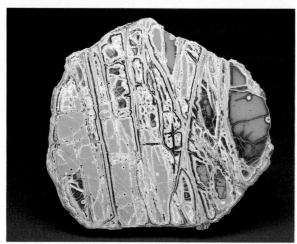

9

10

12. The younger of these two generations of quartz crystals was tinged pink by impurities in the liquid from which the crystals grew.
13. Once mined for ore, the Red Cloud mine in Arizona where this wulfenite occurs is now valuable for its crystals. **14.** These rhodochrosite crystals, sliced from a stalactite, formed from slowly dripping manganese-rich water.

11

12

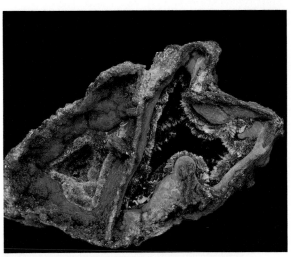

13

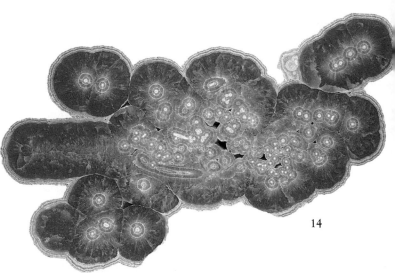

14

15. Eighteenth-century Chinese jadeite altar bowls were used during marriage ceremonies.
16. A perfect sphere, this magnificent quartz crystal ball is almost 13 inches in diameter and weighs almost 107 pounds.
17. Muscovite crystals formed at each end of an exceptionally large and fine specimen of blue beryl (aquamarine) from Pakistan.   **18.** The 138-carat Rosser Reeves ruby is a star of the museum's collections, in every sense.

19. With its checkered history and rumored curse, the Hope Diamond remains the most popular of the museum's gems.
20. Despite its menacing popular name, little is known about the history of the emerald and diamond Spanish Inquisition necklace.
21. Surrounding 36 matched emerald-cut sapphires from Sri Lanka, 435 diamonds reflect some of their light into the blue stones.

15

16

17

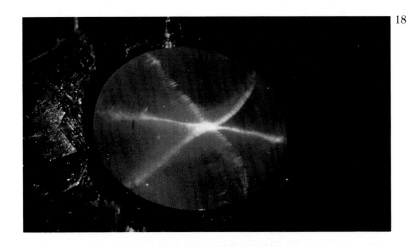

18

19

20

21

THE HUMAN CONNECTION

❧

MAN DID NOT WEAVE THE WEB OF LIFE,
HE IS MERELY A STRAND IN IT.
WHATEVER HE DOES TO THE WEB, HE DOES TO HIMSELF.

❧

CHIEF SEATTLE

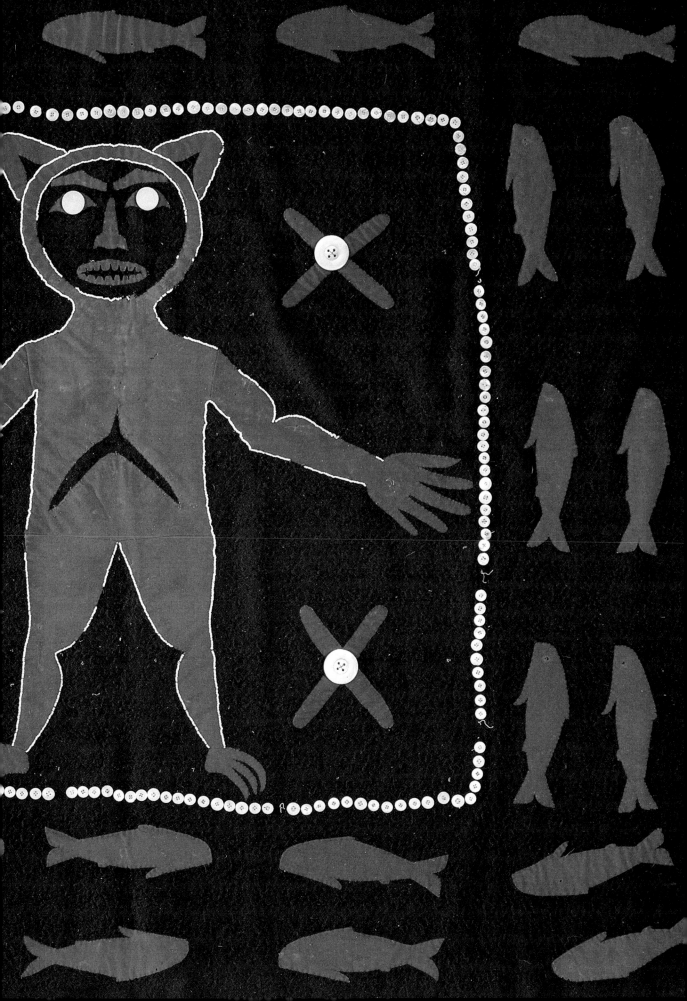

FROM THE FIRST SHARP CHIPS FLAKED FROM A FLINT PEBBLE IN ANCIENT AFRICA TO THE TINIEST SILICA CHIP EMBEDDED IN A SPACE-AGE COMPUTER, THE ABILITY TO CREATE HAS ENABLED HUMANS TO SURVIVE.

TODAY OVER 5 BILLION PEOPLE ARE DISPERSED ACROSS THE GLOBE, EACH CULTURAL GROUP ADAPTING TO ITS HUMAN AND NATURAL ENVIRONMENT. WAYS OF SURVIVING AND THRIVING ARE THE RICH SUBJECTS OF THE MUSEUM'S CULTURAL RESEARCH, COLLECTIONS, AND EXHIBITS.

HOW DO PEOPLE WORK, PLAY, AND WORSHIP? WHAT IS ART FOR? HOW AND WHEN DID AMERICA'S FIRST PEOPLE ARRIVE? HOW CAN A LIVABLE FUTURE RESPECT THE ENVIRONMENT AND CULTURAL NEEDS?

SEARCHING THE MUSEUM TO ANSWER THESE QUESTIONS, YOU'LL ENCOUNTER CULTURAL SOLUTIONS ANCIENT AND CONTEMPORARY. WE HOPE THAT YOU ALSO DISCOVER SOMETHING ABOUT YOURSELF, AND LEAVE BETTER ABLE TO UNDERSTAND YOUR OWN CONNECTIONS TO THE HUMAN AND NATURAL WORLD. ᘓ

1

PRECEDING PAGES: The figure in this Tsimshian flannel-appliqued button blanket may represent a salmon chief. In Tsimshian myth, each salmon species has its own chief and village beneath the sea. 🐟

1. Modern humans are shown at the top of John Gurche's "Tower of Time" as part of the long, ever-changing sequence of life on earth.

2. A kayak model is surrounded by darts, harpoon heads, and a seal scratcher—tools of Bering Sea seal hunters.

3. The Easter Islanders of the South Pacific erected monumental statues as memorials to the dead. **4.** A bronze figurine of Rim-Sin, king of the Mesopotamian city state of Larsa, ca. 1800 B.C., is inscribed with a Sumerian prayer.

5. A clay economic tablet written in cuneiform is enclosed in a clay envelope impressed with signature seals.

6. The ancient Egyptians often mummified and buried sacred animals such as this cat.

7. A diorama in the Ice Age hall takes you to France 70,000 years ago as Neandertal people buried a young man, along with stone tools and bear meat. **8.** In a Bronze Age cemetery in Jordan, this tomb contained the skeletons of an adult man, two children, and an infant.

9. A bronze "spirit boat" lamp from Sardinia documents trade links the Etruscans forged with the Mediterranean world.

10. The inner and outer mummy coffins of a high priestess of the god Amon-Ra (ca. 1000 B.C.) are elaborately painted in mythic scenes. **11.** A bronze sword from Luristan, Iran, was made by a warlike culture dated to around 1000 B.C.

6

7

8

9

10

11

12. An Athenian coin from 480-400 B.C. shows the head of Athena on one side, with an owl and olive branch on the reverse. **13.** These artifacts suggest the richness of African craftsmanship and the diversity of African cultures. **14.** A diorama in the African Cultures hall re-creates a dancing scene following Luvale boys' initiation into manhood.

15. A brass and copper Kuta mortuary image from west-central Africa symbolizes a deceased ancestor or a deity from the land of the dead. **16.** This 15th-century brass head from the West African kingdom of Benin memorialized a queen mother. **17.** This West African brass hornblower dating from the 16th to 18th centuries shows European influence.

12

13

14

18. Painted Grecian pottery often recorded scenes from Greek military history and athletic competitions, as on this vase showing a discus thrower. **19.** This Phoenician glass bottle from Cyprus shows iridescence caused by centuries of weathering in damp surroundings.

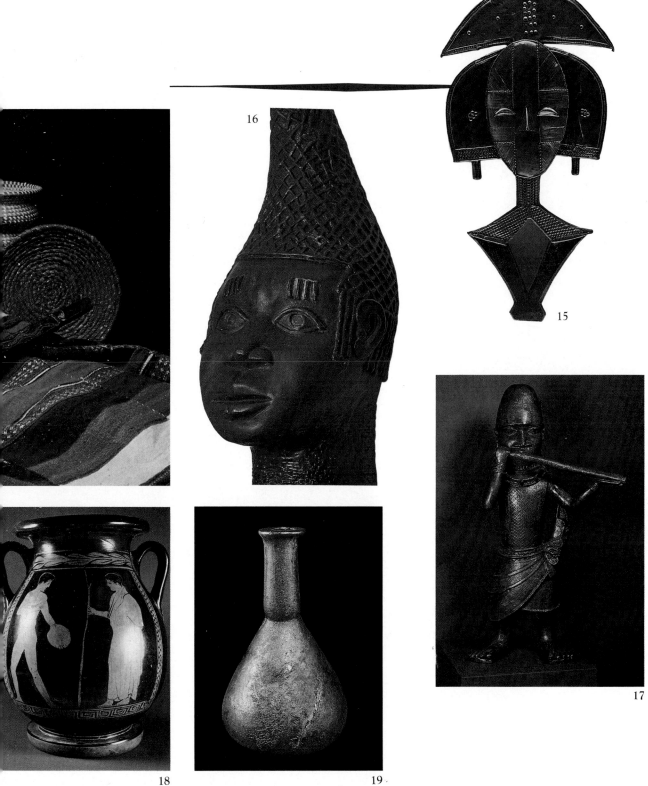

15

16

17

18

19

20. Relying on elaborate costuming, Chinese drama combines singing, to express the characters' feelings, with spoken dialogue, to relate the play's action. **21.** Ivory Coast carvings are both good-luck fetishes and portrait figures. **22.** Fijian chiefs exchanged yards and yards of decorated bark cloth by wearing it to the ceremonial presentation. **23.** This Kuba mask from southern Zaire portrays Mashamboy, a phantom who punishes unruly women and children with a terrible sickness. **24.** A cast-iron Sakyamuni Buddha, from 11th-century Korea, was a gift of the government and people of the Republic of Korea.

20

21

22

25. The South American hall puts cultural objects in the context of the environments in which their makers lived: in the foreground two tropical forest habitats are re-created. **26.** Inside the Plains Indian tipi, the host sat opposite the doorway with male guests to his left and his wife and female guests to the right. **27.** Called the Key Marco cat, this intriguing six-inch wooden figurine was made by Calusa Culture carvers at least six hundred years ago in Florida. **28.** Tehuelche hunters take aim at a rhea (a relative of the ostrich) in this South American hall diorama. **29.** Plains Indian warriors dressed in their finest clothing for battle. This war shirt is decorated with beadwork, feathers, and fringes of human hair. **30.** Navajo silversmiths (ca. 1880) melted coins, cast basic shapes in stone or metal molds, and then hammered and decorated the pieces by hand. **31.** This Sioux chief's eagle feather bonnet (ca. 1880) contains 77 eagle feathers, along with beadwork, trade cloth, and white weasel skin.

25

26

27

28

29

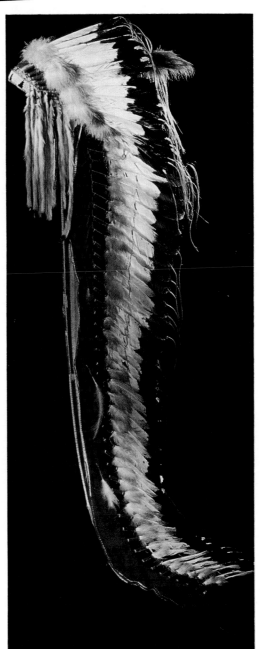

30

32. A Tlingit wooden war helmet in the shape of a scowling warrior's head once bristled with bear fur and human hair. **33.** Before they acquired horses, Indians of the northwestern plains hunted buffalo by driving them over a cliff.
34. A mythical creature decorates the interior of this bent wood food tray from western Alaska.
35. This Kwakiutl dance mask of the Cannibal society represents the Hokhokw, a giant man-eating bird.

33

34

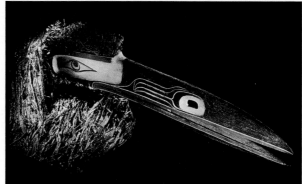

35

32

36. This drawing, made by Sitting Bull, portrays the chief himself in battle, pointed out by a line drawn from the sitting buffalo in the upper right. **37.** This mask from the Lower Yukon River represents the spirit, or inua, of the Bear, in this case meant to be a grizzly. **38.** Zuni pottery is built by hand with coils of clay; this jar is decorated with black and red designs on white slip. **39.** Pomo basket makers of California sometimes decorated gift baskets with natural bird feathers and shell beads.

36

38

37

39

THIS PLACE FOR DISCOVERY

❧

A CREATURE WITHOUT MEMORY CANNOT
DISCOVER THE PAST,
ONE WITHOUT EXPECTATION CANNOT CONCEIVE A FUTURE.

❧

GEORGE SANTAYANA

Whether you are a visitor to the Insect Zoo, finding that you can hold a hissing cockroach without wincing, or a staff scientist bent over an electron scanning microscope, everyone is a discoverer here.

In the museum's molecular systematics lab, DNA researchers are decoding basic notes of the organic symphony. In mineralogy labs, crystallographers are delving into the precise geometric arrangements of atoms that underlie the entire inorganic world. And in southern California's surf, biologists are diving in to examine and record changes in fragile coral reefs.

You can sample this scientific process by participating in Discovery Room and Naturalist Center programs, or you can simply roam our halls, searching for the exotic or chancing on some wonderful fact about the ordinary that gives it new meaning for you. ❧

DISCOVERY ROOM

PRECEDING PAGES: Meet the beetles! With nearly 300,000 species described—about six times as many as all vertebrates—beetles are the most numerous and most diverse of insects. 🐛 **1.** Visitors of all ages flock to the Discovery Room to look *and* touch. **2.** Moving in for a closer look, boys examine a snake preserved in alcohol. **3.** The Discovery Room's "discovery boxes" encourage everyone to be a scientist—to touch, examine, and explore the natural world. **4.** Amateur naturalists over the age of 12 can take advantage of the Naturalist Center's more than 28,000 diverse specimens. **5.** Bridging the gap between specimens on display and the millions of objects in research collections, the Naturalist Center offers the chance to study natural history specimens firsthand. **6.** Naturalist Center visitors may use scientific instruments, consult references, watch videotapes, and follow self-learning guides.

2

3

5

4

6

7. A century and a half of field work has yielded millions of specimens and artifacts, from which new information can be gleaned and against which it can be measured. **8.** Before a fossil can be studied or a complete skeleton makes its appearance in an exhibit, it must be removed from the surrounding rock, cleaned, and chemically stabilized if necessary. **9.** Research at the molecular systematics laboratory includes studies on the evolutionary history of flowering plants and the dynamics of natural hybridization.

10. A diver collects coral off the Caribbean island of Mayaguana, to be used in the living Coral Reef exhibit. **11.** Precisely drawn by senior scientific illustrator George Venable, this carabid beetle is not only beautiful but an important tool used in identifying other specimens. **12.** Entomologists work late in Bolivia. The number of new insect species they've identified has dramatically changed our perception of how many there are.

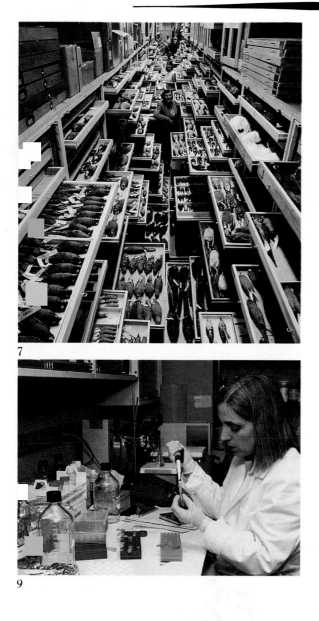

7

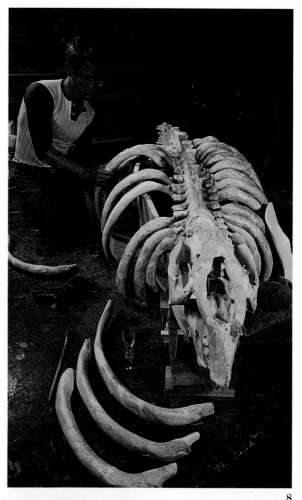

8

10

9

13. In North Carolina's Outer Banks, zoologists collect sea mammals that wash up on shore to study the animals' biology, determine the cause of death, and add specimens to our collections.

14. A museum anthropologist researches pottery made by Native Americans and African Americans used on colonial plantations, such as these vessels from the Catawba Indians of South Carolina.

11

12

13

14

15

15. The tropical leaf insect's near-perfect camouflage protects it from natural predators such as birds. **16.** One of the largest members of the giant silk moth family, the Atlas moth has clear spots, or "windows," on its wings.
17. This tree-climbing caterpillar of a giant silkworm moth really gets a grip with its extra long prolegs as it feeds on leaves and stems.
18. The black and yellow argiope spider's web is an aerial trap for flying prey.

16

17

18

19

19. Cone-headed katydids blend in well with their surroundings, and feast on small insects and nuts. **20.** High-speed photography captures a katydid in mid-leap, revealing how the insect uses its legs and wings in unison to jump.
21. Weevils can be very destructive beetles, boring into stems, fruit, and seeds to lay eggs.
22. The bite of most tarantula species is no more dangerous to humans than a bee sting.

23. The giant water bug male carries eggs glued onto his back by the female, keeping them wet for over a week until they hatch as nymphs.

20

22

21

23

A *Picture Tour of the National Museum of Natural History* was created by the Book Development division, Smithsonian Institution Press, in conjunction with the National Museum of Natural History: Stan Shetler, Assistant Director for Programs; Robert D. Sullivan, Associate Director for Public Programs; Sue Voss, Writer/Editor.

Book Development division staff:

Caroline Newman, *Executive Editor;*

Paula Dailey, *Picture Editor;*

Heidi Lumberg, *Assistant Editor.*

The editors would like to thank their colleagues at the Smithsonian who helped create this book: Judy Blake, Peter Cannell, Alan Carter, Jennifer Clark, Linda Deck, Linda Eisenhart, Richard Fiske, Kathleen Gordon, Francis Hueber, Margaret Jackson, Jill Johnson, Elizabeth Klafter, Sally Love, Vichai Malikul, Jay H. Matternes, Laura McKie, Larry O'Reilly, Rafael Pena, Felicia Pickering, Jeffrey Post, Robert Robbins, Rusty Russell, Ray Rye, Phil Savoire, Peter Sawyer, Theresa Singleton, D.A. Swanson, Alice Tangerini, George Venable, Scott Willett, and the Office of Printing and Photographic Services.

Special thanks to Mr. Brewer.

Special thanks also to the National Aquarium in Baltimore, especially Vicki Aversa and Jack Cover.

Book Design by The Watermark Design Office

Special photography by Chip Clark; additional photography by Dane Penland, Mark Gulezian/Quicksilver.

5 4 3 2 1

95 94 93 92 91

Library of Congress Cataloging-in-Publication Data
National Museum of Natural History (U.S.)

A picture tour of the National Museum of Natural History/ text by Robert D. Sullivan and Sue Voss ; special photography by Chip Clark.

   p. cm.

  ISBN 1-56098-050-8

  1. National Museum of Natural History (U.S.)—Pictorial works.

2. National Museum of Natural History (U.S.)—Guide-books.
I. Sullivan, Robert D., 1949- . II. Voss, Sue. III. Clark, Chip.
IV. Title.

QH70.U62W75 1991   91-1979

508'.074753—dc20   CIP

∞ The paper used in this publication meets the minimum requirements of the American National Standard for Permanence of Paper for Printed Library Materials Z39.48-1984.

Magnificent Haida and Tsimshian carved cedar totem poles, collected in the Pacific Northwest over one hundred years ago, soar into the Constitution Avenue lobby stairwell.